W9-BMB-576

 OCEANS ALIVE!

On The Seabed

BROWN BEAR BOOKS

Published by Brown Bear Books Limited

An imprint of
The Brown Reference Group Ltd
68 Topstone Road
Redding
Connecticut
06896
USA
www.brownreference.com

ISBN-13: 978-1-933834-64-1

Printed in the United States of America

For The Brown Reference Group Ltd
Project Editor: Tom Jackson
Designer: Lynne Lennon
Picture Researcher: Sean Hannaway
Indexer: Tom Jackson
Design Manager: David Poole
Managing Editor: Tim Harris
Production Director: Alastair Gourlay
Children's Publisher: Anne O'Daly
Editorial Director: Lindsey Lowe

Contents

Introduction

If all the water in the oceans drained away overnight, we would see the most spectacular landscape on Earth.

★ Echo-sounders are used to map the seabed's features hidden beneath the waves.

Hidden world

People can only stay in the deep ocean for a short time, and so few explorers have visited the seafloor. However, we have made maps of the seabed. Without water, the ocean floor would be a vast plain. Every so often, ranges of flat-topped mountains would rise up with steep canyons cutting into their sides. In other places there would be terrifyingly steep valleys plunging down thousands of feet.

★ IN DEEP WATER

Sailors find the depth of the ocean beneath them using an echo-sounder. This machine fires pulses of sound down through the water and then measures the time the pulse takes to bounce back off the bottom. The longer the pulse takes to come back, the deeper the water is.

4

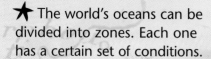

★ The world's oceans can be divided into zones. Each one has a certain set of conditions.

All the way down

The seafloor stretches from just below low-tide level, to the bottom of ocean trenches. The deepest trenches are more than 33,000 feet (10,000 meters) below the surface. Near the coasts, the seafloor gradually slopes away from the continents. These regions are known as **continental shelves**. They are sometimes hundreds of miles wide.

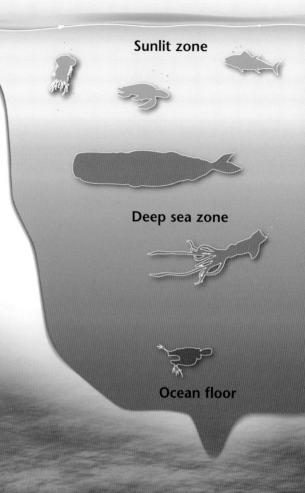

Tidal zone

Sunlit zone

Deep sea zone

Ocean floor

Your Mission

You are going to investigate the seafloor, from the shallow continental shelf to the deepest parts of the seafloor.

Off the shelf

The continental shelf slopes gently down until the water is about 1,000 feet (300 meters) deep. At the edge of the shelf, the **continental slope** is much steeper. At the bottom of the slope, the deep seafloor is mainly flat. Most of it is about 10,000 feet (3 km) under the surface.

Sunken treasures

You will start your journey by looking for treasure off the coast of Florida. After that, your journey takes you across the Gulf of Mexico to look at the Mississippi Delta. Then you cross to the Pacific and explore the kelp forests of California.

Arctic

Pacific
Ocean

North
America

① 1

② 2

③ 3

⑤ 5

Equator

④ 4

South
America

Atlantic
Ocean

Places you will visit
1. Florida coast
2. Mississippi Delta
3. Kelp forest
4. East Pacific Rise
5. Gulf of Mexico

★ Octopuses, lobsters, and starfish survive by crawling around on the floor of shallow seas.

Going deep

Moving down the continental slope, your next stop will be to look at the weird wildlife of the deep ocean floor. Then, you will travel south to explore the underwater volcanoes and **hydrothermal vents** of a **midocean ridge**. There, you will see living things that feed on chemicals in the water. Finally, you will dive near the west coast of Mexico to find animals that live on ice! It is going to be an exciting journey.

Sunken Treasure

Off the Atlantic coast of Florida is a series of islands. The islands are made from sand washed up from the seabed by the ocean's most powerful storms—hurricanes!

Stormy weather

The Atlantic hurricane season begins in July. In the past, most sailors would avoid long voyages at that time. But sometimes ships have to travel. On July 24, 1715, a fleet of 12 Spanish ships set sail from Cuba full of gold and silver. The ships were hit by a hurricane. Eleven of them were sunk near the Florida islands. Most of the wrecks have now been found, but a few are still hidden on the sandy seabed. You are going to look for them.

★ Underwater archaeologists have to work fast. Anything they have uncovered will be buried again by the shifting sand in a few hours.

Treasure hunt

The seafloor is just 26 feet (8 meters) down. At first all you find is a pile of rocks. It does not look like a wreck. Then you see a rusted cannon! This must be it. The rocks are the ship's ballast, the weights carried to keep it upright in the water. All the ship's wood has rotted away—but the treasure is still there!

★ These Spanish coins were made from metal mined in South America. The gold coins were *dubloons*, while the silver ones were *reales*.

Sand blower

A pipe is lowered from the boat. It forces out a jet of water that blasts away the sand on the seafloor. As the sand is pushed away, you see some dark disks. Rubbing away the dirt, you reveal writing, and the disks become shiny gold and silver coins. An expert on board the dive boat says they were made in the early 1700s. The undersea haul is worth thousands of dollars!

In the Sand

The sand on the Florida seabed is swept along by an ocean current called the Gulf Stream.

⭐ A pair of flounders are almost impossible to see against the sandy seabed. The flatfish lie hidden waiting for crabs or small fish to come near. Then the two fish attack.

Sink and settle

The Gulf Stream carries tiny fragments of rock that have been worn away from the shore. The heavier bits sink through the water and settle on the seafloor. There, they form banks of sand and gravel. This happens in other coastal seas all over the world.

Eye

← Eye

Shifting sands

The sand banks cover the solid rock of the continental shelf—and anything else on the bottom. Big storms sometimes sweep the sand away and things that have been buried for years are exposed. This is why you found the wreck.

Sample search

You collect a sample of sand away from the wreck. It contains a lot of two-shelled **mollusks** called clams. Clams suck water through their bodies and collect the bits they can eat. There are also worms in the sand. They eat the sand, **digest** any food in it, and then throw out the rest.

★ **Bacteria** are very small. A line of 100,000 would stretch across your fingernail.

★ HIDDEN FOOD

Using a microscope you find tiny living things called bacteria and protists in the sand. They eat bits of dead animals and seaweeds that drift down through the water. Mollusks, worms, and sea urchins eat the bacteria. So, there is a whole wildlife community living on and buried in the sand.

11

River Delta

Some of the sand and mud on the seabed is **sediment** that is washed off the land by a river. You are going to take a look at one of the world's mightiest rivers—the Mississippi.

Land and water

When a river's water meets the ocean, it slows down and falls to the seafloor, forming a **delta**. A delta is a huge fan of mud with a network of river channels running through it.

★ The seawater around the mouth of the Amazon—the world's largest river—is full of mud for hundreds of miles out to sea.

★ **HEAVY LOAD**

The layer of solid rock lying beneath the Mississippi Delta is lower than the rest of the continental shelf. It has been pushed down by the huge weight of the Mississippi's mud

River view

You fly across the Gulf of Mexico to New Orleans, a city located near the Mississippi Delta. From the plane you see a huge muddy swamp spreading south of the city.

Drilling ship

You take a ship down the river to investigate the underwater delta. When you are far from land, the crew drills down through layers of mud and sand. The drill creates long cores of mud and sand, divided into layers. The layers of sediment change as you get out to sea. The river drops heavier sand but the finest mud is carried far out to sea—to the very edge of the continental shelf.

★ Most of the Mississippi's mud is hidden under the sea. The mud covers an area of seabed that is bigger than the state of Louisiana!

★ Scientists figure out the age of the layers of mud in a drill core by studying the **fossils** in them.

Kelp Forest

After the muddy seabed of the Mississippi Delta, you head to California where the seabed is very different—it is covered in a forest!

In the sunshine

The forest is made of a seaweed called kelp. Seaweeds are similar to land plants. They use the energy from sunlight to make sugar out of **carbon dioxide** and water. The process is called **photosynthesis**.

Floating fronds

Most seaweeds are small and grow in shallow water near the shore. California's kelp is different. It can grow to far more than 100 feet (30 meters) tall and grows out to sea in the deeper water above the continental shelf. The great green **fronds** of the kelp are like leaves. The fronds have gas-filled bags which make them float.

★ Giant kelp is the fastest growing plant in the world. It can grow 2 feet (61 cm) in one day!

Rich water

The giant kelp creates a thick underwater forest for two reasons. The water is very clear so a lot of light reaches the seabed. The water is also rich in the **nutrients** that are drawn up from the deep ocean to the continental shelf by the California Current, which flows south from Alaska.

★ Kelp forests provide food and shelter for many animals, such as this starfish.

Weedy haven

Sea anemones and crabs gather around the kelp stems. Sea snails and sea slugs glide over the fronds looking for food. Swimming through the kelp are many fish, mostly **camouflaged** to hide among the kelp. There is also a larger animal hiding down there. It is a giant octopus that is bigger than you are!

San Francisco

USA

①

Places you will dive
1. Kelp forest
2. East Pacific Rise

Mexico

Gulf of Mexico

● Acapulco

Pacific Ocean

②

Smashing Time

While you are exploring the kelp, you discover that you are not the only **mammal** swimming in the forest.

Forest hunter

The kelp forest is the winter hunting ground for sea lions. One swoops out of the fronds as it looks for a squids, crabs, or young octopuses. In summer, this sea lion will head to the rocky shore to breed. As you follow the sea lion up to the surface, another diving mammal paddles past. This one is a sea otter.

★ Sea lions stay in kelp forests because they can hide there from their worst enemy —the great white shark.

★ Sea otters have some of the thickest fur of any animal. The fine hairs keep their skin dry even when they are diving to the seabed.

★ After feeding, a sea otter might take a nap floating on the surface. It anchors itself to one place as it sleeps by wrapping itself in kelp.

Shell cracker

The sea otter is diving to the seabed to collect a sea urchin or shellfish. After snatching up an abalone, the otter picks up a flat stone. You both head to the surface, and as you watch, the sea otter floats on its back with the stone on its chest. It takes the abalone in both paws and smashes it open against the stone. Then the otter scoops out the flesh.

17

On the Edge

It is now time you took a look at the seabed in deeper water. You head to the continental slope, where the seafloor plunges down into the deep ocean.

Sponge reef

Your ship now travels out to sea, away from the kelp forests to the edge of the continental shelf. The water is about 660 feet (200 meters) deep here, and the seabed is covered in sponges. It is too deep to **scuba** dive so you visit the bottom in a **submersible**.

Dark water

Only a little light makes it down this deep. It is too dark for plants. Things living down here must catch all their food. You spot a glass sponge. Most sponges are springy, but glass sponges have brittle skeletons made from a glassy mineral called **silica**.

★ Glass sponges suck seawater through their hollow bodies to collect food.

Land

Canyon →

18

Down the slope

When a glass sponge dies, its skeleton stays on the rock. New sponges grow on top, making a reef. The sponge reef lies beside the continental slope. This is a gentle slope with deep canyons cut into it. Its underwater cliffs plunge down for thousands of feet.

The cliffs are covered with animals. For example, see-through sea squirts cling to the rocks. Shoals of fish swim along the cliffs, feeding on its inhabitants. Out in the gloom you see larger hunters—squids are coming to attack the fish.

★ They may not look like it, but sea squirts (right) are more closely related to humans than they are to jellyfish, corals, or sponges.

★ This computer image (below) shows the narrow continental shelf along the coast of south California, around Los Angeles.

Continental Shelf

Continental Slope

Deep and Dark

You spend the next day sailing south to the East Pacific Rise. This area of seabed west of Mexico is the start of a chain of underwater mountains that stretches to Antarctica.

Long dive

You dive the submersible to the abyssal plain at the bottom of the continental slope. It takes two hours to reach the bottom. The seabed is a long way down—2.5 miles (4 km) below the surface. It is pitch dark in the deep ocean. The only natural light is the soft glow of **bioluminescent** animals that swim past.

★ Sea cucumbers eat the mud on the seabed and digest any food in it. They have a circle of tentacles around their head for shoveling mud into their mouth.

★ Spider crabs search the seabed for dead fish that have sunk from the water above.

Life in the mud

The sub hovers just above the cream-colored mud of the ocean floor. At first there is not much to see. Then you notice what looks like a bumpy slug moving across the mud, leaving a trail behind it. It is a sea cucumber.

Seafloor slitherer

Sea cucumbers are common seabed animals. They are related to starfish and sea urchins. If one is under attack, a sea cucumber turns its stomach inside out and squirts it out from its bottom! That is enough to scare off predators.

Fire and Water

After returning to the surface, you set off south, sailing over the East Pacific Rise. You are heading for a volcano hidden among the underwater mountains.

Ripped rocks

The East Pacific Rise is a crack in Earth's surface created as its crust is ripped apart. As the rocks split, hot **lava** bursts out. The lava cools into rock called **basalt**. This forms the underwater mountains either side of the crack.

★ LITTLE BY LITTLE

The seafloor is spreading very slowly between the two ridges of the East Pacific Rise. In the Atlantic Ocean, this spreading effect is slowly pushing North and South America away from Europe and Africa at the rate of about 1 inch (2.5 cm) every year

Up and over

You take the submersible up one side of the mountains to look at the crack in the middle of the ridge. The high peaks are covered with gray-brown mud. Then the seafloor gets deeper and becomes bare rock formed into strange round blobs.

★ Red-hot lava erupts from an undersea volcano. It is cooled very rapidly by the water.

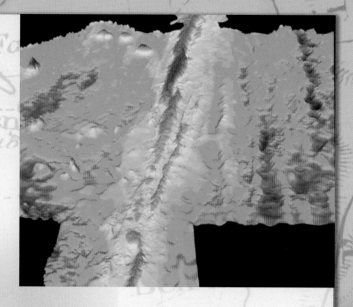

★ A **sonar** map of the East Pacific Rise shows the mountains either side of the crack in Earth's crust.

Young ground

The bare rock has not been on the seafloor long enough to get covered in mud yet. It must be much newer than the muddy peaks above it. This is where all Earth's rock comes from. It bubbles out of Earth's hot insides from cracks like this ocean ridge.

In action

The submersible has reached a part of the ridge where lava is still coming out of the seafloor. You see a flash of red, and hot, thick lava squirts out like glowing toothpaste from a tube. The red turns to black almost immediately as the lava cools into one of the blobs. But then the blob bursts open and more lava squirts out of the side, making yet another blob. These strings of blobs are called pillow lavas.

Deep Heat

Ocean water gets into cracks in the ridge and is heated by the hot rocks. When it is squirted out again, the water is mixed with chemicals that feed some of the weirdest creatures on Earth.

In hot water

The jets of hot water are called hydrothermal vents. You cannot see one in the dark, but your computer shows you that an area of warm water is in front of you. Suddenly, the water heats up very quickly. The lights of the submersible pick out a column of what looks like black smoke. The "smoke" is pouring out of a ragged-looking rock tower.

★ CHEMICAL DIET 🐟

A tubeworm has no mouth or gut, and its body is packed with bacteria. The bacteria make food from the chemicals that pour out of the black smoker. The worm supplies the bacteria by gathering the chemicals with its gills. In return, the worm feeds on some of the bacteria.

★ Tubeworms collect nutrients from the water by waving their red, feathery **gills**.

Smoke in the water

The smoky water is an amazing 700 °F (370 °C). It could melt the sub's plastic windows, so you keep your distance. Just a few feet from the vent, the water is a comfortable 70 °F (21°C). As the water cools, the chemicals dissolved in it turn into tiny specks. These specks are the "smoke" given off by the vents. The hottest vents give out black smoke.

Life support

You would expect the hot water in the vent to kill everything near it. But the black smoker in front of you is is surrounded by mussels and giant clams, with shells as big as footballs. Giant worms also live in tubes around the vent. They are as tall as a person and as thick as a man's wrist.

★ Hydrothermal vents that produce white "smoke" are cooler than black smokers. The vent mixes with cold water underground.

Cold Seep

Now that you have seen the hottest places on the seabed, it is time to look at one of the coldest. For this you must transfer to a ship in the Gulf of Mexico.

Eating chemicals

Bacteria that make food from chemicals in the water use a process called **chemosynthesis**. The animals living around the black smoker survive on the food made in this way. Other seabed animals make use of the chemicals in ice.

★ The ice on the seabed is called methane hydrate. It might be possible to mine this ice and use it as fuel.

Salty sea

You dive 2,000 feet (610 meters) to the seafloor of the Gulf of Mexico. You find tubeworms and large mussels. But there are no black smokers here. A sensor on the submersible measures the salt in the water. It is much saltier than you expect because it is full of a chemical called hydrogen sulfide.

Frozen gas

The hydrogen sulfide seeps out cracks into rocks in the seafloor, along with another chemical called methane. Methane is usually a gas. It burns in air and is used for cooking and heating. Here, on the seafloor of the Gulf of Mexico, it mixes with cold water to form a soft methane ice. Places where this happens are called cold seeps.

Ice worm

Just as around a hydrothermal vent, the tubeworms and mussels are full of chemosynthetic bacteria. The bacteria build food from the hydrogen sulfide in the water. Some tiny worms even burrow through the methane ice. They must be some of the strangest creatures in the ocean.

★ Despite being much colder, seeps are just as crowded with life as any hydrothermal vent.

The Lessons We've Learned

Your exploration of the seafloor has taken you from the sunlit shallow water off the coast of Florida to the deep ocean, where Earth's rocks are formed.

Shallow seas

You have seen how sand and mud from continents make deep sediments on the continental shelf, and how animals live in the sediments. Near Florida, you helped discover the remains of a Spanish treasure ship. Then you explored a kelp forest on the California coast and met some of the animals that make it their home.

★ Sponges are perhaps the simplest type of animal. They have been living on the seabed for more than half a billion years.

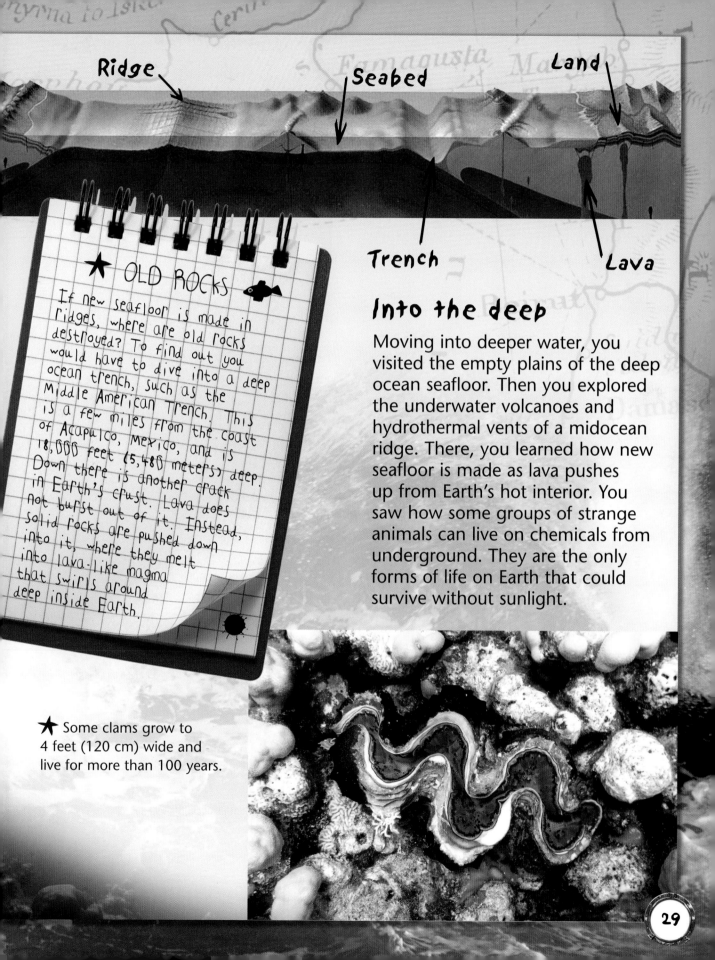

Ridge

Seabed

Land

Trench

Lava

★ OLD ROCKS 🐟

If new seafloor is made in ridges, where are old rocks destroyed? To find out you would have to dive into a deep ocean trench, such as the Middle American Trench. This is a few miles from the coast of Acapulco, Mexico, and is 18,000 feet (5,480 meters) deep. Down there is another crack in Earth's crust. Lava does not burst out of it. Instead, solid rocks are pushed down into it, where they melt into lava-like magma that swirls around deep inside Earth.

Into the deep

Moving into deeper water, you visited the empty plains of the deep ocean seafloor. Then you explored the underwater volcanoes and hydrothermal vents of a midocean ridge. There, you learned how new seafloor is made as lava pushes up from Earth's hot interior. You saw how some groups of strange animals can live on chemicals from underground. They are the only forms of life on Earth that could survive without sunlight.

★ Some clams grow to 4 feet (120 cm) wide and live for more than 100 years.

Glossary

bacteria very tiny living things that multiply by splitting in two

basalt dark rock. Most of the seafloor is made from basalt

bioluminescent describes living things that produce light

camouflaged has particular colors or shape that makes it difficult to see

carbon dioxide heavy, colorless gas that animals produce when they use energy. Plants use carbon dioxide to make food from sunlight.

chemosynthesis process that uses the energy from chemical reactions to make sugar from water and carbon dioxide

continental shelf gently sloping edge of a continent that is covered by a shallow sea

continental slope area leading down from the submerged edge of a continent to the deep ocean floor

delta landform made when a river dumps mud and other sediment into the ocean

digest break down food so it can be used by the body

fossils remains or traces of long-dead animals and plants that have been preserved in stone

fronds leaflike parts of seaweeds

gills parts of the body used by a water animal for breathing

hydrothermal vents places where hot water spouts up from the rocks

lava rock that is so hot it is liquid. Lava gushes from volcanoes.

mammal warm-blooded, usually furry animal that feeds its young on milk

midocean ridge place where molten rock oozes out to form the seafloor. The rock cools, becomes hard, and makes chains of underwater mountains.

mollusks soft-bodied animals, such as clams and snails, that are often protected by shells

nutrients substances that are needed by animals and plants to stay strong and healthy.

photosynthesis process by which plants use the energy in sunlight to make sugars from water and carbon dioxide

scuba equipment that divers use so that they can breathe underwater

sediment tiny pieces of rock or dead remains that have settled in a layer

silica very hard substance in many rocks. It also forms glass.

sonar device that locates solid objects by detecting reflected sound signals

submersible small submarine craft designed for short trips. Some can dive to great depths.

Further Information

Books

A Journey into the Ocean by Rebecca L. Johnson. Minneapolis, MN: Carolrhoda Books Inc., 2004.

Marine Habitats: Life in Saltwater by Salvatore Tocci. New York, NY: Franklin Watts, 2004.

Oceans: Underwater Worlds by Laura Purdie Salas. Minneapolis, MN: Picture Window Books, 2007.

Web sites

Games and videos from the BBC's Blue Planet site.
http://www.bbc.co.uk/nature/blueplanet/

National Oceanic and Atmospheric Administration Ocean Explorer.
http://oceanexplorer.noaa.gov/

A guide to hydrothermal vents from the Woods Hole Oceanographic Institution.
http://www.divediscover.whoi.edu/vents/index.html

Information about Pacific kelp forests from the Monterey Bay Aquarium.
http://www.montereybayaquarium.org/efc/kelp.asp

Index